Party Cakes

& MORE

FUN FOODS FOR KIDS

Publications International, Ltd.

Acknowledgments

The publisher would like to thank the following companies and organizations listed below for the use of their recipes and photographs in this publication.

Alpine Lace Brands, Inc.
Hershey Foods Corporation
Kraft Foods, Inc.
M&M/MARS

National Honey Board
Nestlé USA, Inc.
The Procter & Gamble Company
Reckitt & Colman Inc.

Microwave Cooking: Microwave ovens vary in wattage. Use the cooking times as guidelines and check for doneness before adding more time.

Contents

Tips & Techniques

At the center of every celebration are creative party foods. Inside you'll find a variety of cakes and treats for birthday and holiday parties. Just follow the helpful tips on the next few pages and you'll be decorating like a professional in no time!

Special Cake Equipment

Some cakes use decorating techniques that may require special cake decorating equipment. The right equipment not only makes decorating easier, but also gives more professional results.

Flexible metal spatulas of various sizes are useful in applying frosting and creating very smooth surfaces.

Wooden toothpicks are useful for marking designs on the cakes.

Paste food colors create vibrant colored frostings and do not thin the frosting like liquid colorings.

Decorating bags are essential for piping decorations. Make sure you have a bag for each color of frosting.

Decorating tips are used to pipe different shapes. Writing, round and open star tips are the most commonly used tips.

A **coupler** inserted into the pastry bag before filling makes changing tips easier.

Cake boards are made of heavy corrugated cardboard that can be covered and cut to fit the cake shape.

A **pastry brush** is used to remove crumbs from unfrosted cakes.

Basic Cake Know-How

The perfect cake for decorating is firm, moist and not crumbly. A freshly baked cake can be difficult to work with so plan to bake the cake one day before you need to decorate it. If time doesn't permit, place the cooled cake in the freezer for 30 to 45 minutes to make it easier to cut, frost and decorate.

THE BEST BAKING PANS
Use shiny metal pans or pans with a nonstick finish. Grease and flour all pans before adding the cake batter.

DIVIDING THE BATTER
When baking layer cakes, it is important to divide the batter equally to make even layers. Either measure the batter and divide it equally or weigh the pans after adding the batter. Spread the batter evenly and tap the pans on the countertop to remove air bubbles before baking.

TESTING FOR DONENESS
Always bake cakes at the oven temperature and for the time specified in the recipe. Test cakes after the shortest time given. A cake is done when a toothpick inserted into the center comes out clean. It should pull away from the sides of the pan and spring back when lightly touched in the center.

COOLING CAKES
Let cakes cool in the pans on wire racks for about 10 minutes. Loosen cake edges with a spatula. Place the rack, top side down, over the pan. Flip the rack and the pan over together and the cake should drop out onto the rack. If it does not come out, tap the bottom of the pan. The cake should come out easily. Remove the pan. Place a second wire rack over the cake and flip both racks and the cake back over so the cake can cool top side up. Remove the top rack. Always cool a cake completely before frosting.

STORING CAKES
Cool cakes completely before covering or storing. If using the undecorated layers within two days, wrap tightly in foil or plastic wrap and store in a cool place. For longer storage, wrap in plastic wrap, then in heavy-duty foil or place in resealable freezer bags; freeze for up to two months. To thaw, remove the layers from the freezer and let them thaw, wrapped, at room temperature.

Before Frosting

COVERING CAKE BOARDS

Cake boards can be covered with foil, greaseproof paper, paper doilies or plastic wrap. To cover, cut the foil or paper 1 to 2 inches larger than the board. Center the board on the reverse side of the paper. Cut slashes in the paper almost to the board along any curved edges. Fold the edges over the board and tape into place. If a cake is very heavy, stack two cake boards together before covering for additional support.

When you are ready to frost the cake, tuck strips of waxed paper underneath the bottom cake layer to keep the plate or covered board clean. When decorating is complete, carefully slide out the strips and touch up frosting as needed.

TRIMMING CAKES

If the tops of the cake layers are rounded, trimming them gives more professional results. Use a serrated knife long enough to cut across the top in one stroke, such as a bread knife. Use a gentle sawing motion as you cut through the cake.

The sides of square or rectangular cakes should also be trimmed to make them more even. Use a soft pastry brush to remove all loose cake crumbs.

CUT-APART CAKES

For cleaner cutting lines and fewer crumbs, place the cake in the freezer for 30 to 45 minutes. Use the diagrams and photos as guides and follow the directions carefully. A ruler and toothpicks are helpful to mark designs and act as guides while cutting.

The Frosting Story

FROSTING CONSISTENCY

The proper frosting consistency is the secret to successful decorating. Frosting should hold its shape when scooped with a spatula. If the frosting is too soft because the kitchen is warm, refrigerate the frosting for about 15 minutes and keep it chilled while you work. If the frosting is soft because liquid coloring was used or too much milk was added, beat in some additional sifted powdered sugar. If the frosting is too stiff, beat in additional milk, a small amount at a time, until the desired consistency is achieved.

BASE FROSTING

Frosting cakes with a base frosting (page 13) is a professional technique that gives the cake a smoother, cleaner finish and makes frosting the cake much easier. Spread a thin layer of base frosting on all sides of the cake after cutting and positioning the layers or pieces. Let the base frosting dry a few minutes before covering it with a thicker layer of final frosting.

FROSTING CUT-APART CAKES

Frosting the pointed pieces of cut-up cakes takes extra care. First, freeze the pointed pieces for at least 30 minutes. If frosting a small piece, hold the piece in your hand. Starting at the point, carefully spread thinned frosting along the side, using long strokes away from the point until all sides are frosted. Frost again with thicker frosting. If the tip of the point needs additional frosting, carefully dab it on with the spatula.

TINTING FROSTING

To get bright colors and to keep the frosting at the proper consistency, tint frosting with paste food colorings. Add a small amount of the paste color with a toothpick, then stir well. Slowly add more color until the frosting is the desired shade. If you use liquid food coloring and your frosting becomes too thin, add additional powdered sugar, beating until the desired consistency is reached.

TINTING COCONUT

Place coconut in resealable plastic food storage bag. Mix a few drops of food coloring with ½ teaspoon water. Add to coconut and close bag. Shake until coconut is evenly coated. Repeat procedure for a darker shade.

Decorating Tip Techniques

USING A DECORATING BAG

Some of the recipes call for piped designs. For each of the techniques, you'll need a decorating bag fitted with the appropriate tip and filled with frosting. If you will be using different tips when decorating, a coupler must be used when changing tips. A coupler is used to attach tips to the decorating bag and allows you to change tips without removing the frosting from the bag. To use, unscrew the ring. Insert the cone-shaped piece into the narrow end of an empty decorating bag until the narrow end extends slightly beyond the end of the decorating bag (snip off the end of the decorating bag if necessary). Place the coupler ring over the decorating tip. Screw the ring on to hold the tip in place. To change tips, unscrew the ring, remove the tip, replace with the new tip and screw the ring back in place.

To fill a decorating bag, insert the decorating tip or attach the tip with a coupler. Fold the top of the bag down, then use a spatula to place the frosting in the bag. In general, fill the bag half to two-thirds full, then unfold the top of the bag. Twist the top of the bag tightly against the frosting.

Place twisted end of the bag in the palm of your writing hand. Position fingers near the opening of the bag. Position other hand under bag to guide tip as shown.

When piping, hold the bag so the tip is at the angle indicated for the technique. Then, gently squeeze to force the frosting out, using even pressure while guiding the tip. Do not loosen your grip on the twisted end or the frosting will begin to push up and out of the top of the bag. Push mainly with the palm of your hand rather than squeezing with your fingers.

Line (use writing or small open star tip): Hold bag so tip is at a 45° angle to the right. While gently squeezing bag, guide tip opening just above cake in a straight, curved, zigzag or squiggly line. To end line, stop squeezing, then lift tip.

Writing (use writing tip): Hold bag so tip is at a 45° angle to the right for horizontal lines and toward you for vertical lines. While gently squeezing bag, guide tip opening just above cake to form print or script letters. Stop squeezing, then lift tip at the end of each letter for print letters and at the end of each word for script writing. To pipe built up writing, start piping letter and then hesitate briefly while still squeezing. When desired amount of frosting has built up, resume gliding tip opening for letter. Try to evenly space the built up areas on the letters.

Dot (use round tip): Hold bag so tip is at a 90° angle. Position opening just above the cake and gently squeeze. Lift slightly while still squeezing. When dot is desired size, stop squeezing, then lift tip. To pipe a dot border, position tip almost touching first dot and pipe another dot. Repeat to complete border.

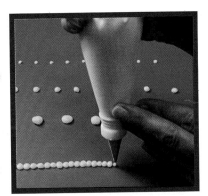

Star (use open or closed star tip): Hold bag so tip is at a 90° angle. Position opening just above cake and gently squeeze. Lift slightly while still squeezing. When star is desired size, stop squeezing, then lift tip. To pipe a star border, position tip almost touching first star and pipe another star. Repeat to complete border.

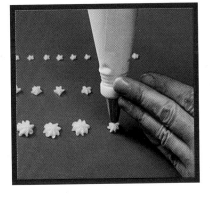

Basic Recipes

Creamy Decorator's Frosting

Makes about 5 cups

1½ cups vegetable shortening
1½ teaspoons lemon, coconut, almond or peppermint extract
7½ cups sifted powdered sugar
⅓ cup milk

Beat shortening and extract in large bowl with electric mixer on medium speed until fluffy. Slowly add ½ of sugar, ½ cup at a time, beating well after each addition. Beat in milk. Add remaining sugar; beat 1 minute more until smooth and fluffy.* Store in refrigerator. (Frosting may be used for frosting cake and/or piping decorations.)

If frosting seems too soft for piping roses or other detailed flowers or borders, refrigerate for a few hours. Refrigerating frosting usually gives better results, but you may also try stirring in additional sifted sugar, ¼ cup at a time, until desired consistency.

Note: This frosting also works well as the base frosting on a cake. Thin frosting by adding a little more milk.

Fluffy White Frosting

Makes about 2 cups frosting

1 container (16 ounces) vanilla frosting
¾ cup marshmallow creme

Combine frosting and marshmallow creme in medium bowl; mix well.

12

Creamy White Frosting

*Makes enough to fill and frost 2 (8-inch) round or square cake layers
or frost 1 (13×9-inch) cake*

½ cup vegetable shortening
6 cups sifted powdered sugar,
   divided
3 tablespoons milk
2 teaspoons clear vanilla
   extract
Additional milk*

**For thinner frosting, use more milk and
for thicker frosting use less milk.*

Beat shortening in large bowl with electric mixer at medium speed until fluffy. Gradually beat in 3 cups sugar until well blended and smooth. Carefully beat in 3 tablespoons milk and vanilla. Gradually beat in remaining 3 cups sugar, adding more milk, 1 teaspoon at a time, as needed for good spreading consistency. Store in refrigerator.

Fudge Frosting

*Makes enough to fill and frost 2 (8-inch) round or square cake layers
or frost 1 (13×9-inch) cake*

24 large marshmallows, halved
⅔ cup semisweet chocolate
   chips
½ cup vegetable shortening
½ cup water
5 cups sifted powdered sugar
3 teaspoons vanilla

Place marshmallows, chocolate, shortening and water in 1½-quart saucepan. Cook over low heat until melted and smooth, stirring constantly. Remove from heat; let stand 5 minutes. Gradually beat in sugar and vanilla with electric mixer at medium speed about 6 minutes or until mixture starts to lose gloss. Use frosting immediately.

Base Frosting

Makes about 2 cups

3 cups powdered sugar, sifted
½ cup vegetable shortening
¼ cup milk
½ teaspoon vanilla
Additional milk

Combine sugar, shortening, ¼ cup milk and vanilla in large bowl. Beat with electric mixer on medium speed until smooth. Add more milk, 1 teaspoon at a time, until frosting is a thin consistency. Use frosting immediately.

White Cake

Makes 2 (8-inch) round or square cake layers or 1 (13×9-inch) cake

2½ cups all-purpose flour
1¾ cups sugar
3 teaspoons baking powder
¼ teaspoon salt
1½ cups milk
½ cup vegetable shortening
2 teaspoons vanilla
4 egg whites

Preheat oven to 350°F. Combine flour, sugar, baking powder and salt in large bowl. Add milk, shortening and vanilla. Beat with electric mixer on low speed 30 seconds or until well blended, scraping side of bowl once. Beat on high speed 2 minutes, scraping side of bowl occasionally. Add egg whites; beat 2 minutes more, scraping bowl once. Grease and flour bottoms and sides of 2 (8-inch) round or square cake pans or 1 (13×9-inch) cake pan. Pour batter evenly into pans.

Bake 30 to 35 minutes for 8-inch round or square cakes or 35 to 40 minutes for 13×9-inch cake. Cakes are done when toothpick inserted into centers comes out clean. Cool in pans on wire racks 10 minutes. Loosen sides of cake layers from pans with knife or metal spatula. Remove to wire racks; cool completely.

Chocolate Cake

Makes 2 (8-inch) round or square cake layers or 1 (13×9-inch) cake

2 cups sugar
1⅔ cups all-purpose flour
½ cup unsweetened cocoa powder
1 teaspoon baking powder
½ teaspoon baking soda
¼ teaspoon salt
1 cup buttermilk
½ cup vegetable shortening
1 teaspoon vanilla
3 eggs

Preheat oven to 350°F. Combine sugar, flour, cocoa, baking powder, baking soda and salt in large bowl. Add buttermilk, shortening and vanilla. Beat with electric mixer on low speed 30 seconds or until well blended, scraping side of bowl once. Beat on high speed 2 minutes more, scraping side of bowl occasionally. Add eggs; beat 2 minutes more, scraping bowl once. Grease and flour 2 (8-inch) round or square cake pans or 1 (13×9-inch) cake pan. Pour batter evenly into pans.

Bake 30 to 35 minutes for 8-inch round or square cakes or 35 to 40 minutes for 13×9-inch cake. Cakes are done when toothpick inserted into centers comes out clean. Cool in pans on wire racks 10 minutes. Loosen sides of cake layers from pans with knife or metal spatula. Remove to wire racks; cool completely.

Note: To prepare 10- and 12-inch cake layers, see Note on page 15.

Yellow Cake

Makes 2 (8-inch) round or square cake layers or 1 (13×9-inch) cake

2½ cups all-purpose flour
1¾ cups sugar
2½ teaspoons baking powder
¼ teaspoon salt
1⅓ cups milk
½ cup butter or margarine, softened
2 teaspoons vanilla
3 eggs

Preheat oven to 350°F. Combine flour, sugar, baking powder and salt in large bowl. Add milk, butter and vanilla. Beat with electric mixer on low speed 30 seconds or until well blended, scraping side of bowl once. Beat on high speed 2 minutes more, scraping bowl often. Add eggs; beat 2 minutes more, scraping bowl once. Grease and flour 2 (8-inch) round or square cake pans or 1 (13×9-inch) cake pan. Pour batter evenly into pans.

Bake 30 to 35 minutes for 8-inch round or square cakes or 35 to 40 minutes for 13×9-inch cake. Cakes are done when toothpick inserted into centers comes out clean. Cool in pans on wire racks 10 minutes. Loosen sides of cake layers from pans with knife or metal spatula. Remove to wire racks; cool completely.

Note: To prepare 10- and 12-inch layers, double ingredients and prepare batter as directed. Grease and flour 1 (10-inch) and 1 (12-inch) cake pan. Pour batter into cake pans, filling each half full. (You will need more batter in 12-inch pan.) Bake 35 to 40 minutes for 10-inch cake and 40 to 45 minutes for 12-inch cake. Cakes are done when toothpick inserted into centers comes out clean. Cool as directed. Repeat procedure with another double batch of cake batter for second 10- and 12-inch cake layers.

Butter Cookie Dough

Makes about 3 cups dough

¾ cup butter or margarine, softened
¼ cup granulated sugar
¼ cup packed light brown sugar
1 egg yolk
1¾ cups all-purpose flour
¾ teaspoon baking powder
⅛ teaspoon salt

1. Combine butter, granulated sugar, brown sugar and egg yolk in medium bowl. Add flour, baking powder and salt; mix well.

2. Cover; refrigerate about 4 hours or until firm.

Unforgettable Birthday Cakes

Corky the Clown

Makes 16 to 18 servings

CAKES & FROSTINGS
    1 (9-inch) square cake
    1 (9-inch) round cake
    3 cups Buttercream Frosting
        (recipe follows)*
    1 recipe Base Frosting
        (page 13) (optional)
    Orange, yellow and pink
        paste food coloring

**DECORATIONS &
EQUIPMENT**
    1 (19×13-inch) cake board,
        covered
    Pastry bags, medium
        writing tip and star tip
    Assorted candies

*Color ³⁄₄ cup frosting orange, ¹⁄₂ cup yellow and ¹⁄₄ cup pink; reserve 1¹⁄₂ cups white frosting.

1. Trim tops and sides of cakes. Cut square cake as shown in diagram 1.

2. Position pieces on prepared cake board as shown in diagram 2, connecting pieces with some of the Buttercream Frosting.

3. Frost entire cake with Base Frosting to seal in crumbs, if desired.

4. Frost face with Buttercream Frosting. Using writing tip and pink frosting, pipe mouth.

5. Frost bow tie and top of hat with yellow frosting as shown in photo. Frost hat with some of the orange frosting. Using star tip and orange frosting, pipe design on hat and bow tie. Arrange assorted candies as shown.

BUTTERCREAM FROSTING

    6 cups powdered sugar, sifted
        and divided
    ³⁄₄ cup butter or margarine,
        softened
    ¹⁄₄ cup shortening
    6 to 8 tablespoons milk,
        divided
    1 teaspoon vanilla

Combine 3 cups powdered sugar, butter, shortening, 4 tablespoons milk and vanilla in large bowl. Beat with electric mixer until smooth. Add remaining powdered sugar; beat until light and fluffy, adding more milk, 1 tablespoon at a time, as needed for good spreading consistency.

Makes about 3¹⁄₂ cups

Corky the Clown

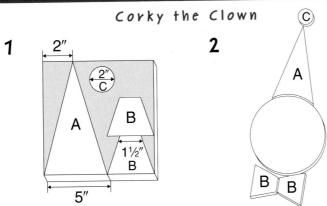

Balloon Cake

With this eye-catching cake, guests at a birthday party or other celebration can have their balloons and eat them too. Decorate the balloons in the favorite colors of the guest of honor.

Makes 16 to 20 servings

CAKE & FROSTINGS
    1 (13×9-inch) cake
    1 recipe Creamy Decorator's
       Frosting (page 12)
      Blue, green and yellow
       paste food coloring
    1 to 2 tablespoons milk
    1 recipe Creamy White
       Frosting (page 13)

EQUIPMENT
    1 (19×13-inch) cake board,
      covered
    4 decorating bags with
      couplers
    Tips: Numbers 2, 4 and 7

1. Trim top and sides of cake. Place cake on prepared cake board.

2. To tint Creamy Decorator's Frosting, tint ¼ cup blue, ¼ cup green, ¼ cup yellow and reserve 1¼ cups for white frosting. Thin remaining Creamy Decorator's Frosting with milk, adding 1 teaspoon at a time, until frosting is a thin consistency.

3. Frost top and sides of cake with thinned frosting to seal in crumbs. Frost again with Creamy White Frosting. Smooth frosting on top and sides.

4. To make balloons, start on left side of cake in center and pipe line in balloon shape with blue frosting and number 4 tip.

5. Pipe dots to completely fill in balloon outline with same frosting and tip as shown in photo 1. (Pipe dots over outline as well.) Repeat to make green and yellow balloons as shown in photo, switching tip with couplers.

6. Carefully smooth surface of dots with damp, not wet, tip of knife as shown in photo 2.

7. Pipe line for center balloon with blue frosting and number 4 tip, piping string straight down. Pipe other strings angled to meet center string with yellow and green frostings, switching tip with couplers.

8. To pipe bow, start at center where strings meet and pipe line in figure 8 with blue and green frostings and number 4 tip.

9. Pipe 1 word in desired writing on each balloon with reserved white frosting and number 2 tip.

10. Pipe bottom and top dot borders with white frosting and switching to number 7 tip. Pipe 3 dots at each corner as border accents with blue, green and yellow frostings and number 4 tip.

Balloon Cake

1

2

Gummy Purple Dinosaur Cake

Of course, dinosaurs can come in other colors, too.

Makes 12 to 16 servings

1 tub (8 ounces) COOL WHIP®
   Whipped Topping, thawed
Few drops blue and red food
   coloring
1 baked 13×9-inch cake, any
   flavor except angel food,
   cooled
Gumdrops
Assorted small candies

TINT whipped topping purple with blue and red food colorings in small bowl with wire whisk.

CUT cake as shown in diagram 1.

USING small amount of whipped topping to hold pieces together, arrange cake on serving tray as shown in diagram 2. Frost cake with remaining whipped topping. Decorate with gumdrops and candies. Serve immediately. Store leftover cake in refrigerator.

Drum Layer Cake

Makes 12 to 16 servings

1 package DUNCAN HINES®
   Moist Deluxe® Cake Mix
   (any flavor)
1 container DUNCAN HINES®
   Creamy Homestyle
   Vanilla Frosting, divided
Green food coloring
Thin pretzel sticks
Candy-coated chocolate
   pieces
Lollipops

1. Preheat oven to 350°F. Grease and flour two 8-inch round cake pans.

2. Prepare, bake and cool cake following package directions for basic recipe.

3. To assemble, place half the Vanilla frosting in small bowl. Tint with green food coloring; set aside. Place one cake layer on serving plate. Spread with half of untinted Vanilla frosting. Top with second cake layer. Spread green frosting on sides of cake. Spread remaining Vanilla frosting on top of cake. Arrange pretzel sticks and candy-coated chocolates on sides of cake. Place lollipops on top of cake for "drumsticks."

> **FUN TIP**
> For brighter green frosting, use paste food colors available from cake decorating and specialty shops.

Gummy Purple Dinosaur Cake

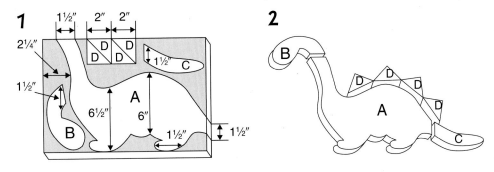

Football Cake

Makes 12 to 16 servings

1 package DUNCAN HINES®
   Moist Deluxe® Devil's
   Food Cake Mix
¾ cup confectioners sugar
2 tablespoons CRISCO® all-
   vegetable shortening
1 tablespoon cold water
1 tablespoon non-dairy
   powdered creamer
¼ teaspoon vanilla extract
   Dash salt
1 container DUNCAN HINES®
   Creamy Homestyle
   Chocolate Frosting

1. Preheat oven to 350°F. Grease and flour 10-inch round cake pan. Prepare cake following package directions for basic recipe. Bake at 350°F 45 to 55 minutes or until toothpick inserted in center comes out clean.

2. Combine sugar, shortening, water, creamer, vanilla and salt in small bowl. Beat at medium speed with electric mixer 2 minutes. Add more sugar to thicken or water to thin frosting as needed.

3. Cut cake according to diagrams 1 and 2, removing 2-inch slice from center. Arrange cake as shown in diagram 3. Spread Chocolate frosting on sides and top of cake. Place basketweave tip in pastry bag. Fill with decorator frosting. Pipe laces.

> **FUN TIP**
> Make 2 football cakes following package directions for 2 (9-inch) round cake pans.

Flower Garden Cake

Makes 16 to 20 servings

1 package DUNCAN HINES®
   Moist Deluxe® Yellow or
   Devil's Food Cake Mix
1 container DUNCAN HINES®
   Creamy Homestyle
   Vanilla Frosting
   Green food coloring
   Mini pretzels
½ teaspoon water
1 cup flaked coconut
   Narrow green ribbon
   Assorted candy suckers

1. Preheat oven to 350°F. Grease and flour 13×9×2-inch pan.

2. Prepare and bake cake following package directions for basic recipe. Cool completely.

3. Tint Vanilla frosting with 3 drops green food coloring. Frost sides and top of cake. Place pretzels upright along top edge to form "fence." Combine water and food coloring in small bowl. Add coconut. Toss with fork until evenly tinted. Sprinkle coconut "grass" over frosting inside pretzel "fence." Tie ribbon bows on each candy sucker stick to form leaves. Arrange assorted sucker "flowers" in "garden."

Football Cake

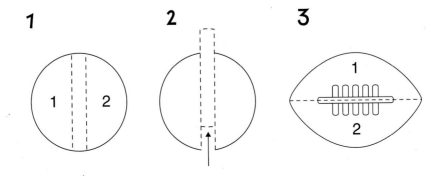

Double Dip Ice Cream Cone Cakes

Serve both cakes for a "double dip," or freeze one for the next occasion.

Makes 12 to 14 servings

1 package (2-layer size) cake mix, any flavor
4 squares BAKER'S® Semi-Sweet Chocolate
¼ cup milk
1 tub (8 ounces) COOL WHIP® Whipped Topping, thawed
Assorted small candies
Multicolored sprinkles
Maraschino cherries

HEAT oven to 350°F.

PREPARE cake mix as directed on package. Divide batter evenly between greased and floured 8-inch round and 8-inch square baking pans. Bake as directed on package. Cool 10 minutes; remove from pans. Cool completely on wire racks.

CUT cakes as shown in diagrams 1 and 2. Assemble pieces on large serving tray as shown in diagrams 3 and 4.

MICROWAVE chocolate and milk in medium microwavable bowl on HIGH 2 minutes or until chocolate is almost melted. Stir until chocolate is completely melted. Cool 20 minutes or until room temperature. Gently stir 1½ cups whipped topping into chocolate with wire whisk until blended.

FROST "cones" with chocolate whipped topping mixture; decorate with candies, if desired. Frost "ice cream" with remaining whipped topping; decorate with sprinkles.

REFRIGERATE until ready to serve. Top with cherries just before serving.

Double Dip Ice Cream Cone Cake

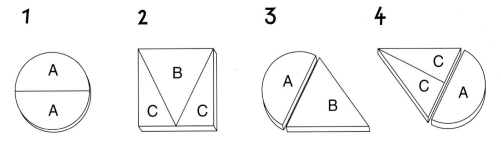

Castle Cake

Make this delightful castle a family project. It's so easy even the youngest members of your kingdom can help decorate it.

Makes 8 to 10 servings

CAKE & FROSTING
   1 (8-inch) square cake
   1 recipe Creamy White
      Frosting (page 13)
      Yellow and blue paste food
      coloring
   1 to 2 tablespoons milk

DECORATIONS & EQUIPMENT
   1 (19×13-inch) cake board,
      covered
   1 (3-inch) peppermint candy
      stick
   ¼ cup sliced natural almonds
   16 red licorice bites
      Tiny multi-colored candies
      and sprinkles

1. Trim top and sides of cake. Cut cake as shown in diagram 1 with serrated knife, using ruler as guide. Freeze pieces 30 to 45 minutes before frosting.

2. To tint frosting, tint 1½ cups bright yellow and ¼ cup bright blue. Thin remaining frosting with milk, adding 1 teaspoon at a time, until frosting is a thin consistency.

3. Position pieces A, B and C on prepared cake board as shown in diagram 2, connecting with some of the yellow frosting. Frost both sides and tops with thinned frosting to seal in crumbs. Frost again with remaining yellow frosting.

4. Hold piece D in left hand. Starting at the point, carefully spread thinned frosting along the side, using long strokes in the direction away from point until all sides are frosted; frost top. Frost again with blue frosting. Position candy stick and blue piece as shown in photo.

5. Decorate with almonds and remaining candy as shown in photo.

Castle Cake

1

1½″

D

B

C

3″

A

3″

2

D

C

B

A

Merry-Go-Round Cake

This makes an ordinary cake into a carousel of fun.

Makes 12 servings

1 package (6-serving size) JELL-O® Instant Pudding and Pie Filling, Vanilla Flavor
1 package (2-layer size) yellow cake mix
4 eggs
1 cup water
¼ cup vegetable oil
⅓ cup BAKER'S® Semi-Sweet Real Chocolate Chips, melted
⅔ cup cold milk
Sprinkles (optional)
Paper carousel roof (directions follow)
3 plastic straws
6 animal crackers

RESERVE ⅓ cup pudding mix. Combine cake mix, remaining pudding mix, eggs, water and oil in large bowl. Beat at low speed of electric mixer just to moisten, scraping sides of bowl often. Beat at medium speed 4 minutes. Pour ½ of the batter into greased and floured 10-inch fluted tube pan. Mix chocolate into remaining batter. Spoon over batter in pan; cut through with spatula in zigzag pattern to marbleize. Bake at 350°F for 50 minutes or until cake tester inserted in center comes out clean. Cool in pan 15 minutes. Remove from pan; finish cooling on rack.

BEAT reserved pudding mix and milk in small bowl until smooth. Spoon over top of cake to glaze. Garnish with sprinkles, if desired.

CUT 10- to 12-inch circle from colored paper; scallop edges, if desired. Make 1 slit to center (diagram 1). Overlap cut edges to form carousel roof; secure with tape (diagram 2). Cut straws in half; arrange on cake with animal crackers. Top with roof.

PREP TIME: 30 minutes
BAKE TIME: 50 minutes

Merry-Go-Round Cake

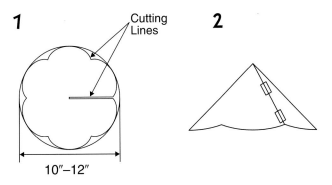

Alphabet Block Cake

Makes 32 to 36 servings

4 (8-inch) square cake layers*

BUTTERCREAM FROSTING
  1 cup butter or margarine, softened
  ⅓ cup shortening
  8 cups (2 pounds) powdered sugar, sifted, divided
  ½ cup plus 2 tablespoons milk, divided
  1 teaspoon vanilla
  Blue food coloring
  Green food coloring
  Jelly (your favorite flavor), melted (about 2½ cups)

DECORATIONS & EQUIPMENT
  1 (19×14-inch) cake board
  Candy-coated chocolate pieces
  Ice cream cone-shaped cookie cutter
  Pastry bag and medium writing tip
  Chocolate sprinkles
  Pink colored sugar

Use your favorite cake recipe or package mix; follow baking instructions for 8-inch square cakes. Two cakes (4 layers) are needed.

1. Trim tops and edges of cakes to make level and of equal size.

2. Beat together butter and shortening; blend in 4 cups powdered sugar, ½ cup milk and vanilla in large bowl. Beat with electric mixer until smooth. Add remaining 4 cups powdered sugar; beat until light and fluffy. Add more milk, 1 tablespoon at a time, as needed for good spreading consistency. Color ¾ cup frosting pastel blue and ¾ cup frosting pastel green; reserve 3 cups white frosting.

3. Cut cake board into 2 (7-inch) squares; stack. Cut remaining board into a 6½-inch square. Place 1 cake layer on 7-inch boards; frost top with ¾ cup white frosting. Top with second cake layer; frost top with ¾ cup white frosting.

4. Place 6½-inch board on top of cake. Top with third cake layer. Frost top with ¾ cup white frosting. Top with fourth cake layer.

5. Cover top and sides of cake with light coating of jelly to seal in crumbs. Frost opposite sides of cake with blue frosting. Frost other 2 sides with green frosting. Frost top of cake with ¾ cup white frosting.

6. Outline edges with chocolate pieces as shown in photo.

7. Using cookie cutter, make outline on top of block. Using writing tip and remaining white frosting, pipe outline of design. Fill with sprinkles and colored sugar.

8. Slice and serve top 2 layers of cake first. To serve bottom section, remove cake board; slice into pieces.

FUN TIP
Personalize cake by adding favorite colors and candies, spelling out child's name in candy or drawing special toy on top of cake.

Alphabet Block Cake

School-of-Fish Cake

Your head will be swimming with compliments when you serve this adorable school of fish. Let your children choose the gumdrop colors for the fish.

Makes 16 to 20 servings

CAKE & FROSTINGS
- 1 (13×9-inch) cake
- 1 recipe Creamy White Frosting (page 13)
- Blue paste food coloring
- 1 recipe Base Frosting (page 13)

DECORATIONS & EQUIPMENT
- 1 (19×13-inch) cake board, covered
- Large and small gumdrops

1. Trim top and sides of cake. Place cake on prepared cake board.

2. Tint Creamy White Frosting blue.

3. Frost top and sides of cake with Base Frosting to seal in crumbs. Frost again with blue frosting. Swirl frosting to resemble waves.

4. To make large fish, position 1 large gumdrop on cutting board and cut lengthwise in half with knife. Set aside 1 gumdrop half for fish body. For tail, place remaining gumdrop half, cut side down, on cutting board. Cut wedge piece from center of wide end as shown in photo 1; set aside.

5. To assemble fish, place fish body in desired position on cake top. Place narrow end of tail piece next to wide end of fish body as shown in photo 2

6. Trim reserved wedge piece into fin shape and place above body of fish.

7. For eyes and bubbles, cut off small pieces of gumdrop and press onto fish and cake. Decorate fish by cutting additional small pieces of gumdrop and pressing pieces onto fish, if desired. Repeat with additional large gumdrops to make more large fish.

8. Repeat with small gumdrops to make small fish.

> **FUN TIP**
> Try experimenting with gumdrops to make a crab or octopus as shown in photo.

School-of-Fish Cake

Baseball Fan Cake

This sporty design is so easy because the hat and bat are made from a cupcake and a cake roll-up.

Makes 16 servings

CAKES & FROSTINGS
- **2 (8-inch) square cakes**
- **1 recipe Creamy Decorator's Frosting (page 12)**
- **Paste food coloring in your team's colors**
- **Brown paste food coloring**
- **1 to 2 tablespoons milk**
- **1 recipe Creamy White Frosting (page 13)**
- **1 purchased cupcake**
- **1 small purchased cream-filled cake roll-up**

EQUIPMENT
- **1 (19×13-inch) cake board, covered**
- **4 decorating bags with couplers**
- **Tips: Numbers 2, 13 or 15, and 30 or 31**

1. Trim tops and sides of cakes.

2. To tint Creamy Decorator's Frosting, tint ¾ cup as desired for primary color of cap, ¼ cup as desired for secondary color of cap, ½ cup light brown and reserve 1 cup for white frosting. Thin remaining Creamy Decorator's Frosting with milk, adding 1 teaspoon at a time, until frosting is a thin consistency.

3. Place one cake on prepared cake board. Frost top with about ½ cup Creamy White Frosting. Place second cake on top. Frost top and sides with thinned frosting to seal in crumbs. Frost again with remaining Creamy White Frosting. Smooth frosting on top and sides.

4. For crown of baseball cap, place cupcake upside down on cake top, positioning about 1 inch from left edge of cake and aligning top edge of cupcake with cake center. Use toothpick to outline bill of cap in frosting.

5. Pipe tiny stars on cupcake and outlined bill with primary color of frosting and number 13 tip, as shown in photo 1.

6. Pipe letter on front of cap with secondary color of frosting and number 2 tip. Pipe large dot for button on top of cap with same frosting and tip.

7. To make bat, cut cake roll-up lengthwise in half. Place 1 piece on angle in upper right corner of cake with rounded side up.

8. Cut remaining piece crosswise in half. Trim sides of 1 half on an angle to resemble grip of bat and place at end of piece on cake, tapered end down. Cut a horizontal slice from bottom of remaining piece and place at tapered end of grip as shown in photo 2.

9. Pipe tiny stars all over bat with brown frosting and number 13 tip. Pipe message in desired writing with secondary color of frosting and number 2 tip.

10. Pipe bottom and top star borders with reserved white frosting and number 30 tip. Pipe small stars and dots as border accents with cap colors and number 13 and number 2 tips.

Baseball Fan Cake

Tugboat Cake

To create a river or lake for your tugboat, use blue plastic wrap to cover the cake board. If you like, crinkle extra plastic wrap and arrange it on board to resemble waves.

Makes 16 to 20 servings

CAKE & FROSTINGS
    1 (13×9-inch) cake
    1 recipe Creamy White
        Frosting (page 13)
        Green, yellow and blue
        paste food coloring
    1 recipe Base Frosting
        (page 13)

DECORATIONS &
EQUIPMENT
    2 (19×13-inch) cake boards
    Blue plastic wrap
    Green, yellow and blue
        sugar (optional)
    1 chocolate sugar wafer
    White or colored candy
        circles
    5 gummy candy circles
    Gummy fish (optional)

1. Trim top and sides of cake. Cut cake as shown in diagram 1 with serrated knife, using ruler as guide.

2. Tint 2 cups Creamy White Frosting green, ¾ cup Creamy White Frosting yellow and ½ cup Creamy White Frosting blue.

3. Stack cake boards and cover with 2 layers of plastic wrap. Position one piece A in center of prepared cake board. Frost top with some of the green frosting. Top with second piece A. Frost top and sides with some of the Base Frosting to seal in crumbs. Frost again with remaining green frosting. Sprinkle top with green sugar, if desired.

4. Frost sides and top of piece B with some of the Base Frosting. Frost again with yellow frosting. Sprinkle with yellow sugar, if desired. Frost sides and top of piece C with Base Frosting. Frost again with blue frosting. Sprinkle with blue sugar, if desired.

5. Position yellow and blue pieces as shown in diagram 2.

6. Cut wafer in half crosswise. Press halves together; place on cake as shown in photo. Decorate with candies as shown.

Tugboat Cake

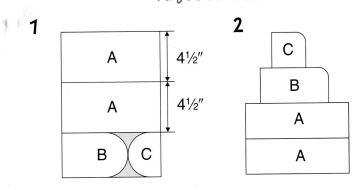

Treasure Chest

Makes 8 servings

1 package (12 ounces)
    ENTENMANN'S® All
    Butter Pound Loaf
1 tub (8 ounces) COOL WHIP®
    Whipped Topping, thawed
    Assorted candies for
    "jewels"
1 pretzel rod, cut into thirds
    Black licorice
2 pretzels

CUT ½-inch slice off top of cake; set aside. Hollow out center of cake, leaving ½-inch shell on bottom and sides. Spoon 1 cup of the whipped topping into cake shell. Frost sides with 1½ cups whipped topping.

REFRIGERATE until ready to serve. Just before serving, place assorted "jewels" over whipped topping in cake shell. Angle reserved cake slice over jewels using pretzel rod pieces to resemble open chest lid. Frost slice with remaining whipped topping. Decorate cake with candies. Add pretzels for handles.

Birthday Extravaganza

Makes 12 to 14 servings

CAKES & FROSTING
    2 (9-inch) round cake layers
    1 recipe Creamy White
        Frosting (page 13)

DECORATIONS &
EQUIPMENT
    1 (10-inch) round cake
        board, covered
    Assorted candies
    Cookie Pops (page 79)
    Rainbows (page 82)
    1 decorating bag
    Tip: Number 31

1. Trim tops of cakes. Place one cake layer on cake board. Frost top with about ½ cup Creamy White Frosting. Place second cake on top. Frost with Creamy White Frosting, reserving 1¼ cups for borders.

2. Sprinkle candies on cake top to resemble confetti. Place Cookie Pops and Rainbows on top of cake.

3. Place remaining 1¼ cups Creamy White Frosting in decorating bag fitted with number 31 tip. To pipe shell border, hold bag at 45° angle just above cake edge at top. Squeeze until small mound is formed for base of shell, lifting slightly. Continue squeezing while pulling tip away from base until desired length. Stop squeezing; lift tip. Position tip almost touching tail of first shell. Repeat technique, completing top and bottom borders. Place candies between shells on bottom border.

Note: For Cookie Pops, use teddy bear, candle, present and balloon cookie cutters. If not available, cut out squares for presents and circles for balloons.

Treasure Chest

Witch Cake

So realistic, this scary cake will be the hit at any child's Halloween party.

Makes 12 servings

INGREDIENTS
1 package (2-layer size) cake mix (any flavor), plus ingredients to prepare mix
2 containers (16 ounces each) cream cheese or vanilla frosting
Green food color
Black decorating gel
Black paste food color
Red string chewy fruit snacks
1 sugar ice cream cone
Assorted candies
Red fruit snack roll-up cutouts

SUPPLIES
1 (15×10-inch) cake board, covered, or large tray
Pastry bag and medium star tip
1 witch's black hat

1. Preheat oven to 350°F. Grease and flour 13×9-inch baking pan.

2. Prepare cake mix according to package directions; pour batter into prepared pan.

3. Bake 30 to 35 minutes or until wooden toothpick inserted into center comes out clean. Cool in pan on wire rack 10 minutes. Remove from pan to rack; cool completely.

4. Place cake on cake board. Spread top and sides of cake with 1 container frosting. Color half of remaining container of frosting with green food color.

5. Trace outline of head onto cake with toothpick. Fill in face with green frosting; outline with decorating gel.

6. Color remaining frosting with black paste food color. Spoon into pastry bag fitted with star tip; pipe frosting around edges of cake.

7. Cut hat in half lengthwise. Place one half on cake; discard remaining half. Place fruit snacks around hat to resemble hair. Decorate face as shown in photo.

Witch Cake

Macho Monster Cake

What fun to decorate a cake that is supposed to look ugly! Make your monster as scary as you can.

Makes 12 servings

INGREDIENTS

1 package (18.25 ounces) cake mix, any flavor, plus ingredients to prepare mix
1 container (16 ounces) cream cheese or vanilla frosting
Green and yellow food color
Black decorating gel
1 white chocolate baking bar (2 ounces)

SUPPLIES

1 (13×9-inch) cake board, covered, or large tray

1. Preheat oven to 350°F. Grease and flour 13×9-inch baking pan.

2. Prepare cake mix according to package directions. Pour into prepared pan.

3. Bake 30 to 35 minutes until wooden toothpick inserted into center comes out clean. Cool in pan on wire rack 10 minutes. Remove from pan to rack; cool completely.

4. Color frosting with green and yellow food color to make ugly monster green as shown in photo. Using diagram 1 as guide, cut pieces out (see Note).

5. Position pieces on prepared cake board as shown in diagram 2, connecting with some frosting. Frost cake. Using decorating gel, pipe eyes, mouth, hair and scars as shown. Break white chocolate baking bar into irregular pieces; position inside mouth as teeth.

Note: For cleaner cutting lines and fewer crumbs, place the cooled cake in the freezer for 30 to 45 minutes before cutting.

FUN TIP

Using the diagram as a guide, draw pattern pieces on waxed paper. Cut pieces out and place them on cake. Cut around pattern pieces with knife. Remove pattern pieces and discard.

Macho Monster Cake

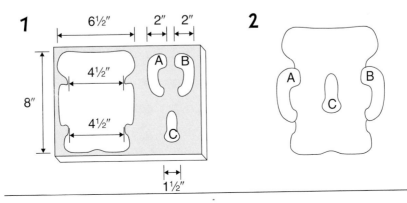

Turkey Cake

Don't expect to have leftovers from this turkey—it's sure to be gobbled up!

Makes 8 to 10 servings

CAKE & FROSTINGS

- 1 (8-inch) round cake layer
- 1 recipe Creamy White Frosting (page 13)
- Red, orange and yellow paste food coloring
- 1 to 2 tablespoons milk
- ½ cup purchased chocolate frosting

DECORATIONS & EQUIPMENT

- 1 (19×13-inch) cake board, covered
- ¼ cup chopped walnuts
- 3 licorice sticks, cut 3 inches long
- 1 thin crosswise slice of licorice stick
- 1 red gummy worm, cut 3 inches long

1. Trim top of cake. Cut cake as shown in diagram 1 with serrated knife. Freeze pieces 30 to 45 minutes before frosting.

2. Tint ½ cup Creamy White Frosting deep red, ½ cup Creamy White Frosting deep orange and ½ cup Creamy White Frosting deep yellow. Thin remaining Creamy White Frosting with milk, adding 1 teaspoon at a time, until frosting is a thin consistency.

3. Hold 1 piece B in left hand. Starting at the point, carefully spread thinned frosting along the side, using long strokes in the direction away from point until all sides are frosted; frost top. Repeat with remaining pieces and thinned frosting to seal in crumbs.

4. Position piece A in center of prepared cake board as shown in photo. Frost sides and top with chocolate frosting. Sprinkle with walnuts.

5. Frost two B pieces with red frosting, two with orange frosting and two with yellow frosting as directed in step 3.

6. Position pieces around piece A as shown in diagram 2.

7. Position licorice and gummy worm as shown in photo.

> ### FUN TIP
> No chocolate frosting on hand? Just tint ½ cup Creamy White Frosting brown with brown paste food coloring.

Turkey Cake

1

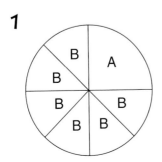

2

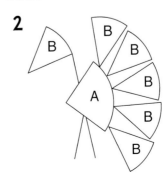

Dreidel Cake

This Hanukkah cake is sure to be a big hit—everyone's a winner with a spin of this dreidel!

Makes 12 servings

INGREDIENTS

- 1 package (2-layer size) cake mix, any flavor
- 1¼ cups water
- 3 eggs
- ¾ cup sliced or slivered almonds, toasted and finely ground*
- ¼ cup vegetable oil
- ½ teaspoon almond extract
- 1½ containers (16 ounces each) cream cheese frosting
- Yellow and blue food colors

SUPPLIES

- 1 large tray or (15×10-inch) cake board, covered
- Pastry bag and medium star tip

To toast almonds, place in single layer on baking sheet. Bake at 350°F for 7 to 10 minutes or until golden brown, stirring occasionally. Cool completely.

1. Preheat oven to 350°F. Grease and flour 13×9-inch baking pan.

2. Combine cake mix, water, eggs, almonds, oil and extract in medium bowl. Beat at low speed of electric mixer until blended. Beat at medium speed 2 minutes. Pour batter into prepared pan.

3. Bake 35 to 40 minutes until wooden toothpick inserted into center comes out clean. Cool in pan on wire rack 10 minutes. Remove from pan; cool completely on rack.

4. Cut cake as shown in diagram 1. Position cake pieces on tray as shown in diagram 2, connecting pieces with small amount of frosting. Frost center of cake with about ½ cup white frosting as shown in photo.

5. Color about ¾ cup frosting yellow; spread onto top and sides of cake as shown in photo.

6. Using diagram 3 as guide, cut out letter; position on cake as shown in photo. Trace around pattern with wooden toothpick; remove pattern. Color remaining frosting blue. Spoon frosting into pastry bag fitted with star tip. Use to fill in letter and pipe around top edge of cake as shown in photo.

Dreidel Cake

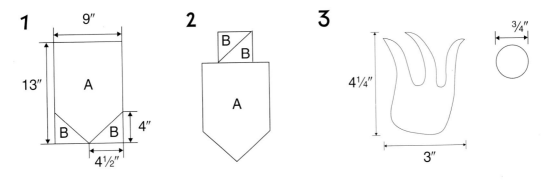

1 9″ 13″ A B B 4″ 4½″

2 B B A

3 4¼″ 3″ ¾″

Chilly Snowman Cake

Make the spirit of winter last for months with this frosty snowman cake.

Makes 12 servings

INGREDIENTS

- 1 package (2-layer size) yellow cake mix, plus ingredients to prepare mix
- 1 cup butter brickle bits
- 22 round peppermint candies
- 1 recipe Cookie Glaze (recipe follows)
- Confectioners' sugar
- 4 frosted mini shredded wheat cereal pieces
- 1 pretzel rod
- 1 recipe Fluffy White Frosting (page 12)
- Coarse sugar (optional)*
- 6 to 8 large marshmallows, divided
- Chewy fruit snack roll
- Red string licorice
- Assorted candies

SUPPLIES

- 1 large tray or (18×10-inch) cake board, covered

Coarse sugar, sometimes called "pretzel sugar," can be found in specialty food stores. Although not necessary for the success of the recipe, it helps add a frosty look to the snowman.

1. Preheat oven to 350°F. Grease and flour one 8-inch round baking pan and one 9-inch round baking pan; set aside.

2. Prepare cake mix according to package directions. Stir in butter brickle bits. Divide batter between prepared pans.

3. Bake 30 to 35 minutes or until wooden toothpick inserted into centers comes out clean. Cool in pans on wire racks 10 minutes. Remove from pans; cool completely on racks.

4. While cakes are cooling, cover baking sheet with foil. Arrange peppermints on prepared sheet to resemble hat as shown in photo. Bake at 350°F 4 to 5 minutes or until mints just begin to melt and stick together. Cool completely.

5. Prepare Cookie Glaze. Stir in enough additional confectioners' sugar to thicken slightly. Using thickened glaze, assemble snowman's broom by "gluing" together shredded wheat pieces and pretzel rod as shown in photo. Let stand until hardened.

6. Arrange cake rounds on tray with smaller round at top of tray. Frost entire cake with Fluffy White Frosting. Sprinkle with coarse sugar, if desired.

7. Place peppermint hat on top of snowman's head. Place 2 marshmallows under hat to support hat on tray, if necessary. Add broom and decorate rest of snowman as shown in photo.

COOKIE GLAZE

- 1 cup confectioners' sugar
- 1 to 1½ tablespoons milk

1. Combine sugar and enough milk to make a medium-thick pourable glaze.

Makes about 1 cup

Chilly Snowman Cake

Candy Cane Cake

Makes 12 to 16 servings

**1 package DUNCAN HINES®
  Moist Deluxe Cake Mix
  (any flavor)**

DECORATOR FROSTING
  5 cups confectioners sugar
  **¾ cup CRISCO® all-vegetable
    shortening**
  ½ cup water
  **⅓ cup non-dairy powdered
    creamer**
  2 teaspoons vanilla extract
  ½ teaspoon salt
    Red food coloring
    **Maraschino cherry halves,
      well drained**

1. Preheat oven to 350°F. Grease and flour 13×9×2-inch pan.

2. Prepare, bake and cool cake following package directions for basic recipe. Remove from pan. Freeze cake for ease in handling.

3. For decorator frosting, combine confectioners sugar, shortening, water, non-dairy powdered creamer, vanilla extract and salt in large bowl.

Beat at medium speed with electric mixer for 3 minutes. Beat at high speed for 5 minutes. Add more confectioners sugar to thicken or water to thin frosting as needed. Reserve 2 cups frosting. Tint remaining frosting with red food coloring.

4. Cut frozen cake and arrange as shown in diagrams 1 and 2. Spread white frosting on cake. Mark candy cane stripes in frosting with tip of knife. Place star tip in decorating bag and fill with red frosting. To make stripes, arrange maraschino cherry halves and pipe red frosting following lines.

∙∙ꞏꞏ FUN TIP ꞏꞏ∙∙

For a quick dessert, serve leftover cake pieces with sugared strawberries and dollops of whipped cream.

Candy Cane Cake

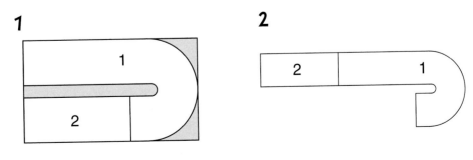

1

2

Angel Cake

This sweet angel is sure to disappear quickly.

Makes 8 to 10 servings

1 (8-inch) round cake layer
1 recipe Creamy White
    Frosting (page 13)
1 to 2 tablespoons milk
5 tablespoons flaked coconut,
    divided
    Red liquid food coloring
1 teaspoon water
2 small blue jelly beans
    Silver edible glitter

Cut cake as shown in diagram 1. Position cake pieces as shown in diagram 2, connecting with frosting. Thin 1½ cups frosting with milk, adding 1 teaspoon at a time, until frosting is of thin consistency. Frost entire cake with thinned frosting to seal in crumbs. Frost with remaining Creamy White Frosting.

Place 4 tablespoons coconut in resealable plastic food storage bag. Combine small amount of food coloring with water; add to bag. Shake until evenly coated. Toast remaining 1 tablespoon coconut in preheated 350°F oven about 5 minutes or until lightly browned. Sprinkle pink coconut on angel's body and toasted coconut on angel's head for hair. Place jelly beans on face for eyes. Sprinkle glitter over angel's wings.

Pretty Pink Heart

Makes 12 to 16 servings

1 package cake mix (2-layer
    size), any flavor except
    angel food
1 cup cold milk
1 package (4-serving size)
    JELL-O® Vanilla Flavor
    Instant Pudding & Pie
    Filling
¼ cup powdered sugar
1 tub (8 ounces) COOL WHIP®
    Whipped Topping, thawed
¼ teaspoon red food coloring
    Multicolored sprinkles

HEAT oven to ? F.

PREPARE cake mix as directed on package. Divide batter evenly between greased and floured 8-inch round and 8-inch square baking pans. Bake as directed on package. Cool 10 minutes; remove from pans. Cool completely on wire racks.

POUR milk into medium bowl. Add pudding mix and sugar. Beat with wire whisk 2 minutes. Gently stir in whipped topping and food coloring.

CUT round cake in half. Place cut sides of round cake along two touching sides of square cake, using pudding mixture to hold pieces together. Frost cake with remaining pudding mixture. Decorate with sprinkles.

Angel Cake

1

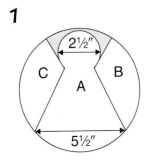

2½"

C   A   B

5½"

2

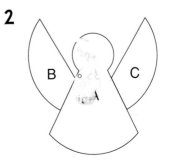

B   C

Hippity Hop Bunny Cake

Surprise the kids after the Easter egg hunt with this cake.

Makes 12 to 16 servings

2¼ cups BAKER'S® ANGEL
    FLAKE® Coconut
Red food coloring
2 baked 9-inch round cake
    layers, cooled
1 tub (8 ounces) COOL WHIP®
    Whipped Topping, thawed
Assorted candies

TINT ¼ cup coconut pink using red food coloring.

LEAVE 1 cake layer whole; cut remaining cake layer as shown in diagram 2. Using small amount of whipped topping to hold pieces together, arrange cake on serving tray as shown in photograph.

FROST cake with remaining whipped topping. Sprinkle center of bunny's ears with pink coconut. Sprinkle remaining 2 cups white coconut over bunny's head and outer edges of ears. Decorate with candies. Store cake in refrigerator.

Lucky Shamrock

Makes 12 to 16 servings

2⅔ cups BAKER'S® ANGEL
    FLAKE® Coconut
Green food coloring
3 baked 9-inch round cake
    layers, cooled
1⅔ cups Vanilla Buttercream
    Frosting (recipe follows)
Green decorating icing

TINT coconut with green food coloring.

LEAVE 1 cake layer whole; cut 1-inch slice from remaining 2 cakes so that cake fits along curve of whole cake.

PREPARE Vanilla Buttercream Frosting. Using small amount of frosting to hold pieces together, arrange whole cake at top of serving tray. Place other 2 cakes along lower edges of whole cake, fitting cut ends along curve. Place 2 small slices between 2 layers as stem.

FROST cake with remaining frosting. Sprinkle with coconut. Using decorating icing, outline the cake.

VANILLA BUTTERCREAM FROSTING

1 package (16 ounces)
    powdered sugar (about
    4 cups)
½ cup (1 stick) margarine or
    butter, softened
3 tablespoons milk
2 teaspoons vanilla

BEAT sugar, margarine, milk and vanilla with electric mixer on low speed until smooth. If frosting becomes too thick, beat in additional milk by teaspoonfuls until of spreading consistency.

Makes about 2½ cups

Hippity Hop Bunny Cake

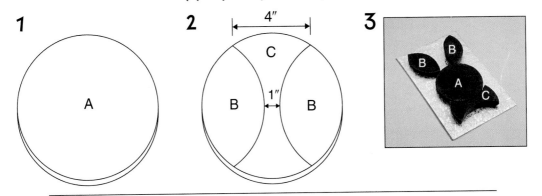

1 A

2 4"
C
B 1" B

3 B B A C

Liberty Bell Cake

Start your 4th of July festivities off with a bang by serving this all-American cake.

Makes 16 servings

CAKE & FROSTINGS
- 1 (13×9-inch) cake
- 1 recipe Creamy White Frosting (page 13)
- 1 recipe Base Frosting (page 13)
- Blue decorating gel

DECORATIONS & EQUIPMENT
- 1 (19×13-inch) cake board, covered
- 1 (1½-inch) star cookie cutter
- Red cinnamon candies

1. Trim top and sides of cake. Cut cake as shown in diagram 1.

2. Position pieces on prepared cake board as shown in diagram 2. connecting with some of the Creamy White Frosting.

3. Frost entire cake with Base Frosting. Frost again with remaining Creamy White Frosting.

4. Gently press cookie cutter into frosting on bell, leaving imprints. Trace outline of imprint with gel. Evenly fill in each star with gel.

5. Decorate with candies as shown in photo.

Flag Dessert

This patriotic dessert is ideal to let the kids decorate!

Makes 15 servings

- 2 pints fresh strawberries
- 1 package (12 ounces) ENTENMANN'S® All Butter Pound Loaf, cut into 16 slices
- 1⅓ cups blueberries
- 1 tub (12 ounces) COOL WHIP® Whipped Topping, thawed

SLICE 1 cup strawberries; set aside. Halve remaining strawberries; set aside.

LINE bottom of 12×8-inch glass baking dish with 8 cake slices. Top with 1 cup sliced strawberries, 1 cup blueberries and ½ whipped topping. Place remaining cake slices over whipped topping. Spread remaining whipped topping over cake. Arrange strawberry halves and remaining ⅓ cup blueberries over whipped topping to create a flag design.

REFRIGERATE until ready to serve.

Liberty Bell Cake

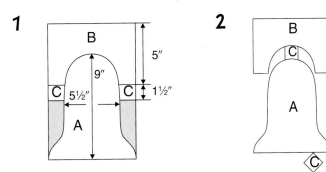

1

B

5″

9″

C 5½″ C 1½″

A

2

B

C

A

◇C◇

Sweet Treats for Festive Occasions

Pumpkin Candy Brownies

Makes 26 brownies

**1 package DUNCAN HINES®
    Chocolate Lovers' Double
    Fudge Brownie Mix
2 eggs
⅓ cup water
¼ cup CRISCO® Oil or
    CRISCO® PURITAN® Oil
1 cup DUNCAN HINES®
    Creamy Homestyle
    Chocolate Frosting
26 pumpkin candies
½ cup DUNCAN HINES®
    Creamy Homestyle
    Vanilla Frosting
Green food coloring**

1. Preheat oven to 350°F. Line 26 (2-inch) muffin cups with foil liners or place on baking sheets.

2. Combine brownie mix, contents of fudge packet from Mix, eggs, water and oil in large bowl. Stir with spoon until well blended, about 50 strokes. Fill each foil liner with 2 level measuring tablespoons batter. Bake 15 to 17 minutes or until firm. Cool 5 to 10 minutes in pans. Remove to cooling racks.

3. Place Chocolate frosting in small saucepan. Melt on low heat, stirring constantly. Frost top of 1 warm brownie with generous ½ teaspoonful melted frosting. Top with 1 pumpkin candy; push down slightly. Repeat for remaining brownies. Cool completely.

4. Tint Vanilla frosting with green food coloring. Place in decorating bag fitted with small leaf tip. Pipe 3 leaves around each pumpkin candy. Use small writing tip to pipe vines, if desired.

Pumpkin Candy Brownies

Halloween Cookie Pizza

Makes about 16 to 20 servings

¾ cup packed light brown sugar
½ cup butter flavor shortening
1 egg
1 tablespoon water
1 teaspoon vanilla extract
1¼ cups all-purpose flour
½ teaspoon baking soda
¼ teaspoon salt
1 cup REESE'S® Peanut Butter Chips
1 cup miniature marshmallows
½ cup HERSHEY₅S Semi-Sweet Chocolate Chips
½ cup chopped pecans
Chocolate Drizzle (recipe follows)
Orange Drizzle (recipe follows)

1. Heat oven to 350°F. Lightly grease 12-inch round pizza pan.

2. In large bowl, beat brown sugar and shortening until creamy. Add egg, water and vanilla; beat well. Stir together flour, baking soda and salt; add to sugar mixture, beating on low speed of electric mixer until well blended. Stir in peanut butter chips. Spread batter into prepared pan to within ½ inch of edge.

3. Bake 11 to 13 minutes or until set. Remove from oven. Sprinkle marshmallows, chocolate chips and pecans over top. Return to oven. Bake 5 to 7 minutes or until marshmallows are lightly browned. Cool completely.

4. Prepare Chocolate Drizzle and Orange Drizzle. Drizzle Chocolate Drizzle over top. Drizzle Orange Drizzle over chocolate. Let stand about 1 hour until drizzles set. Cut into wedges.

Chocolate Drizzle: In small microwave-safe bowl, place ¼ cup HERSHEY₅S Semi-Sweet Chocolate Chips and 1½ teaspoons butter flavor shortening. Microwave at MEDIUM (50%) 1 minute; stir. If necessary, microwave at MEDIUM an additional 15 seconds at a time, stirring after each heating, just until chips are melted when stirred.

Orange Drizzle: In small bowl, stir together ½ cup powdered sugar, 1 tablespoon water, 3 drops yellow food color and 2 drops red food color; stir until well blended.

Turkey Cupcakes

Cupcakes are always a welcome treat
for kids. These are sure to
command a repeat performance!

Makes 2 dozen cupcakes

INGREDIENTS
1 **package (2-layer size) cake
   mix (any flavor), plus
   ingredients to prepare
   mix**
1 **container (16 ounces)
   chocolate frosting**
¾ **cup marshmallow creme**
24 **shortbread ring cookies**
48 **small red candies
   Decorations: candy corn,
   assorted candies**

SUPPLIES
24 **regular-size (2½-inch)
   paper muffin cup liners**

1. Preheat oven to 350°F. Line 24
muffin cups with paper muffin
cup liners.

2. Prepare cake mix according to
package directions. Spoon batter
into prepared muffin pans.

3. Bake 15 to 20 minutes or until
wooden toothpick inserted into
centers comes out clean. Cool in
pans on wire racks 10 minutes.
Remove to racks; cool completely.

4. Combine frosting and
marshmallow creme in medium
bowl; mix well. Frost cupcakes
lightly with frosting mixture;
reserve remaining frosting
mixture.

5. Cut cookies in half. Cut half of
them in half again to form
quarters.

6. For each cupcake, place larger
cookie piece cut-side down on
back edge of cupcake for tail.
Place 1 of the 2 smaller cookie
pieces cut-side down on opposite
side of cupcake for head; discard
remaining smaller cookie piece or
reserve for another use. Frost
cookies with remaining frosting
mixture so they blend in with
cupcake.

7. Position candies on heads for
eyes. Decorate tops of tails with
candies as desired.

Jolly Peanut Butter Gingerbread Cookies

Makes about 6 dozen cookies

1⅔ cups (10-ounce package) REESE'S® Peanut Butter Chips
¾ cup (1½ sticks) butter or margarine, softened
1 cup packed light brown sugar
1 cup dark corn syrup
2 eggs
5 cups all-purpose flour
1 teaspoon baking soda
½ teaspoon ground cinnamon
¼ teaspoon ground ginger
¼ teaspoon salt

1. In small microwave-safe bowl, place peanut butter chips. Microwave at HIGH 1 to 2 minutes or until chips are melted when stirred. In large bowl, beat melted peanut butter chips and butter until well blended. Add brown sugar, corn syrup and eggs; beat until light and fluffy.

Stir together flour, baking soda, cinnamon, ginger and salt. Add half of flour mixture to butter mixture; beat on low speed of electric mixer until smooth. With wooden spoon, stir in remaining flour mixture until well blended. Divide into thirds; wrap each in plastic wrap. Refrigerate 1 hour or until dough is firm enough to roll.

2. Heat oven to 325°F.

3. On lightly floured surface, roll 1 dough portion at a time to ⅛-inch thickness; with floured cookie cutters, cut into holiday shapes. Place on ungreased cookie sheet.

4. Bake 10 to 12 minutes or until set and lightly browned. Cool slightly; remove from cookie sheet to wire rack. Cool completely. Frost and decorate as desired.

Snowmen

Makes 1 dozen cookies

1 package (20 ounces) refrigerated chocolate chip cookie dough
1½ cups sifted powdered sugar
2 tablespoons milk
Assorted small candies

1. Preheat oven to 375°F. Cut dough into 12 equal sections. Divide each section into 3 balls: large, medium and small.

2. For each snowman, place 3 balls in a row, ¼ inch apart, on

ungreased cookie sheet. Repeat with remaining dough. Bake 10 to 12 minutes or until edges are very lightly browned. Cool 4 minutes on cookie sheets. Remove to wire racks; cool completely.

3. Mix powdered sugar and milk in medium bowl until smooth. Pour over cookies. Let cookies stand 20 minutes or until set. Decorate to create faces, hats and arms with assorted candies.

Jolly Peanut Butter Gingerbread Cookies

Conversation Heart Cereal Treats

Makes 12 bars

2 tablespoons margarine or butter
20 large marshmallows
3 cups frosted oat cereal with marshmallow bits
12 large conversation hearts

1. Line 8- or 9-inch square pan with aluminum foil, leaving 2-inch overhangs on 2 sides. Generously grease or spray with nonstick cooking spray.

2. Melt margarine and marshmallows over medium heat 3 minutes or until melted and smooth; stir constantly. Remove from heat.

3. Add cereal; stir until completely coated. Scrape into prepared pan and press evenly onto bottom using greased rubber spatula. Press candies into top of treats while still warm, evenly spacing to allow 1 candy per bar. Let cool 10 minutes. Using foil overhangs as handles, remove treats from pan. Cut into 12 bars.

Valentine's Day Cookie Cards

Create your own Valentine's Day message for that special valentine.

Makes 1 dozen cookies

INGREDIENTS
1 recipe Butter Cookie Dough (page 15)
1 container (16 ounces) vanilla frosting
1 container (16 ounces) pink cherry-flavored frosting
Assorted candies

SUPPLIES
Pastry bags and assorted decorating tips

1. Preheat oven to 350°F. Grease cookie sheets.

2. On lightly floured surface, roll out cookie dough to ⅛-inch thickness. Cut out 4½×3-inch rectangular cookies or use heart-shaped cookie cutter. Place on prepared cookie sheets.

3. Bake 8 to 10 minutes or until edges are lightly browned. Remove to wire racks; cool completely.

4. Spread cookies with desired frostings; spoon remaining frostings into pastry bags fitted with decorating tips. Decorate cookies with frostings and candies to resemble Valentine's Day cards.

Conversation Heart Cereal Treats

Shamrock Ice Cream Sandwiches

Use other holiday-shaped cookie cutters and color the dough the appropriate color.

Makes 6 to 8 cookie sandwiches

INGREDIENTS
1 recipe Butter Cookie Dough (page 15)
3 or 4 drops green food color
1 pint softened ice cream or frozen yogurt, any flavor

SUPPLIES
3½- to 5-inch shamrock-shaped cookie cutter

1. Prepare cookie dough; mix in food color. Cover; refrigerate until firm, about 4 hours or overnight.

2. Preheat oven to 350°F.

3. Roll dough on floured surface to ¼-inch thickness. Cut out cookies using cookie cutter. Place on ungreased cookie sheets.

4. Bake 8 to 10 minutes or until cookies are lightly browned around edges. Remove cookies to wire racks; cool completely.

5. Remove ice cream from freezer; let stand at room temperature to soften slightly, about 10 minutes. Spread 4 to 5 tablespoons ice cream onto flat sides of half of the cookies. Place remaining cookies, flat sides down, on ice cream; press cookies together lightly.

6. Wrap each sandwich in foil; freeze until firm, about 2 hours or overnight.

St. Patrick's Parfaits

They'll all be wearing the green with this fun-to-make, fun-to-eat dessert.

Makes 4 servings

2 cups cold milk
1 package (4-serving size) JELL-O® Pistachio Flavor Instant Pudding and Pie Filling
Chocolate sauce
2 cups thawed COOL WHIP® Whipped Topping
Chocolate shamrock cutouts (optional)

POUR milk into large bowl. Add pudding mix. Beat with wire whisk 1 to 2 minutes.

LAYER pudding, chocolate sauce and 1 cup whipped topping alternately in 4 parfait glasses. Garnish with remaining whipped topping and chocolate shamrock cutouts. Refrigerate until ready to serve.

Shamrock Ice Cream Sandwiches

Frosted Easter Cut-Outs

Makes about 3½ dozen cookies

COOKIES
- **1¼ cups granulated sugar**
- **1 Butter Flavor* CRISCO® Stick or 1 cup Butter Flavor* CRISCO® all-vegetable shortening**
- **2 eggs**
- **¼ cup light corn syrup or regular pancake syrup**
- **1 tablespoon vanilla**
- **3 cups all-purpose flour (plus 4 tablespoons), divided**
- **¾ teaspoon baking powder**
- **½ teaspoon baking soda**
- **½ teaspoon salt**

ICING
- **1 cup confectioners' sugar**
- **2 tablespoons milk**
- **Food color (optional)**
- **Decorating icing**

*Butter Flavor Crisco is artificially flavored.

1. Place sugar and shortening in large bowl. Beat at medium speed of electric mixer until well blended. Add eggs, syrup and vanilla; beat until well blended and fluffy.

2. Combine 3 cups flour, baking powder, baking soda and salt. Add gradually to shortening mixture, beating at low speed until well blended.

3. Divide dough into 4 equal pieces; shape each into disk. Wrap with plastic wrap. Refrigerate 1 hour or until firm.

4. Heat oven to 375°F. Place sheets of foil on countertop for cooling cookies.

5. Sprinkle about 1 tablespoon flour on large sheet of waxed paper. Place disk of dough on floured paper; flatten slightly with hands. Turn dough over; cover with another large sheet of waxed paper. Roll dough to ¼-inch thickness. Remove top sheet of waxed paper. Cut into desired shapes with floured cookie cutter. Place 2 inches apart on ungreased baking sheet. Repeat with remaining dough.

6. Bake one baking sheet at a time at 375°F for 5 to 7 minutes or until edges of cookies are lightly browned. *Do not overbake.* Cool 2 minutes on baking sheet. Remove cookies to foil to cool completely.

7. For icing, combine confectioners' sugar and milk; stir until smooth. Add food color, if desired. Stir until blended. Spread icing on cookies; place on foil until icing is set. Decorate as desired with decorating icing.

Frosted Easter Cut-Outs

Color-Bright Ice Cream Sandwiches

Makes about 24 ice cream sandwiches

¾ cup (1½ sticks) butter or margarine, softened
¾ cup creamy peanut butter
1¼ cups firmly packed light brown sugar
1 large egg
1 teaspoon vanilla extract
1½ cups all-purpose flour
1 teaspoon baking soda
¼ teaspoon salt
1¾ cups "M&M's"® Chocolate Mini Baking Bits, divided
2 quarts vanilla or chocolate ice cream, slightly softened

Preheat oven to 350°F. In large bowl cream butter, peanut butter and sugar until light and fluffy; beat in egg and vanilla. In medium bowl combine flour, baking soda and salt; blend into creamed mixture. Stir in 1⅓ cups "M&M's"® Chocolate Mini Baking Bits. Shape dough into 1¼-inch balls. Place about 2 inches apart on ungreased cookie sheets. Gently flatten to about ½-inch thickness with fingertips. Place 7 or 8 of the remaining "M&M's"® Chocolate Mini Baking Bits on each cookie; press in lightly. Bake 10 to 12 minutes or until edges are light brown. Do not overbake. Cool about 1 minute on cookie sheets; cool completely on wire racks. Assemble cookies in pairs with about ⅓ cup ice cream; press cookies together lightly. Wrap each sandwich in plastic wrap; freeze until firm.

Star Spangled Snack

Makes 8 servings

1 package (4-serving size) JELL-O® Brand Berry Blue Flavor Gelatin
1 package (4-serving size) JELL-O® Brand Gelatin, any red flavor
2 cups boiling water
1 cup cold water
1 tub (8 ounces) COOL WHIP® Whipped Topping, thawed

DISSOLVE each package of gelatin completely in 1 cup boiling water in separate bowls.

Stir ½ cup cold water into each bowl of gelatin. Pour each mixture into separate 8-inch square pans. Refrigerate at least 3 hours or until firm. Cut gelatin in each pan into ½-inch cubes.

SPOON blue cubes evenly into 8 dessert dishes. Cover with whipped topping. Top with red cubes. Garnish with remaining whipped topping.

REFRIGERATE until ready to serve.

Color-Bright Ice Cream Sandwiches

Bunch O' Balloons

You could use sugar cookie dough instead of chocolate chip in this recipe if you wish. These fun cookies could also be decorated to be Halloween pumpkin cookies or holiday ornament cookies.

Makes 8 servings

1 package (20 ounces) refrigerated chocolate chip cookie dough
1 tub (8 ounces) COOL WHIP® Whipped Topping, thawed
Assorted fruits and candies
Decorating gel
Red string licorice

HEAT oven to 350°F.

SLICE cookie dough evenly into 8 slices. Pat each slice into 5-inch circle on lightly floured surface. Place 2 inches apart on ungreased cookie sheets.

BAKE 10 to 12 minutes or until lightly browned. Remove from cookie sheets. Cool completely on wire racks.

SPREAD whipped topping evenly onto each cookie. Decorate with fruit, candy and gel. Arrange decorated cookies on large serving tray to resemble a bunch of balloons. Place a piece of licorice at bottom edge on each cookie to resemble string. Tie strings together with additional licorice. Serve immediately.

Bunch O' Balloons

Letters of the Alphabet

Makes about 5 dozen cookies

1 recipe Gingerbread Cookie Dough (recipe follows) Colored frostings and glazes, colored sugars, sprinkles and assorted small candies

1. Prepare Gingerbread Cookie Dough. Cover; refrigerate about 8 hours or until firm.

2. Preheat oven to 350°F. Grease cookie sheets.

3. Divide dough into 4 equal sections. Reserve 1 section; refrigerate remaining 3 sections.

4. Roll reserved dough on floured surface to ⅛-inch thickness. Sprinkle with flour to minimize sticking, if necessary.

5. Transfer dough to 1 corner of prepared cookie sheet. Cut out letter shapes using 2½-inch cookie cutters. Repeat steps with remaining dough.

6. Bake 6 to 8 minutes or until edges begin to brown. Remove cookies to wire racks; cool completely.

7. Decorate cookies with frostings, glazes, colored sugars, sprinkles and assorted small candies.

GINGERBREAD COOKIE DOUGH

**½ cup shortening
⅓ cup packed light brown sugar
¼ cup dark molasses
1 egg white
½ teaspoon vanilla
1½ cups all-purpose flour
1 teaspoon ground cinnamon
½ teaspoon baking soda
½ teaspoon salt
½ teaspoon ground ginger
¼ teaspoon baking powder**

1. Beat shortening, brown sugar, molasses, egg white and vanilla in large bowl at high speed of electric mixer until smooth.

2. Combine flour, cinnamon, baking soda, salt, ginger and baking powder in small bowl. Add to shortening mixture; mix well. Cover; refrigerate about 8 hours or until firm.

Magic Dip

Makes 6 to 8 servings

**1 package (8 ounces) PHILADELPHIA BRAND® Cream Cheese, softened
1 cup BAKER'S® Semi-Sweet Real Chocolate Chips
½ cup BAKER'S® ANGEL FLAKE® Coconut, toasted
½ cup chopped peanuts**

SPREAD cream cheese on bottom of 9-inch microwavable pie plate or quiche dish.

TOP with remaining ingredients.

MICROWAVE on MEDIUM (50%) 3 to 4 minutes or until warm. Serve with graham crackers. Garnish, if desired.

Letters of the Alphabet

Cookie Cups

Makes 12 cookie cups

1 package (20 ounces) refrigerated sugar cookie dough
All-purpose flour (optional)
Prepared pudding, nondairy whipped topping, maraschino cherries, jelly beans, assorted sprinkles and small candies

1. Grease 12 (2¾-inch) muffin cups.

2. Remove dough from wrapper according to package directions. Sprinkle dough with flour to minimize sticking, if necessary.

3. Cut dough into 12 equal pieces; roll into balls. Place 1 ball in bottom of each muffin cup. Press dough halfway up sides of muffin cup, making indentation in center of dough.

4. Freeze muffin cups 15 minutes. Preheat oven to 350°F. Bake 15 to 17 minutes or until golden brown. Cookies will be puffy. Remove from oven; gently press indentation with teaspoon.

5. Return to oven 1 to 2 minutes. Cool cookies in muffin cups 5 minutes. Remove to wire racks; cool completely.

6. Fill each cookie cup with desired fillings. Decorate as desired.

Giant Cookie Cups Variation: Grease 10 (3¾-inch) muffin cups. Cut dough into 10 pieces; roll into balls. Complete recipe according to regular Cookie Cup directions.
Makes 10 giant cookie cups

FUN TIP

Add some pizzazz to your cookie cups by filling with a mixture of prepared fruit-flavored gelatin combined with prepared pudding or nondairy whipped topping.

Frozen Fudge Pops

Makes 6 to 8 fudge pops

2 cups milk
⅓ cup honey*
3 tablespoons unsweetened cocoa powder
2 tablespoons cornstarch
1 teaspoon vanilla
1 teaspoon butter or margarine

Honey should not be fed to infants under one year of age. Honey is a safe and wholesome food for older children.

Combine milk, honey, cocoa, cornstarch, vanilla and butter in medium saucepan. Cook and stir over low heat until little bubbles appear and mixture thickens. Remove from heat; cool slightly and pour into popsicle molds. Freeze 2 to 4 hours or until firm. Store in freezer.

Favorite recipe from **NATIONAL HONEY BOARD**

Cookie Cups

Dirt Cups

This kid-pleasing favorite can also be made
in a clean, new flower pot and
decorated with lollipop "flowers."

Makes 8 to 10 servings

1 package (16 ounces)
   chocolate sandwich
   cookies
2 cups cold milk
1 package (4-serving size)
   JELL-O® Chocolate Flavor
   Instant Pudding & Pie
   Filling
1 tub (8 ounces) COOL WHIP®
   Whipped Topping, thawed
8 to 10 (7-ounce) paper or
   plastic cups
   Suggested garnishes:
   gummy worms or other
   gummy candies, candy
   flowers, chopped peanuts,
   granola

Crush cookies in zipper-style
plastic food storage bag with
rolling pin or in food processor.

Pour cold milk into large bowl.
Add pudding mix. Beat with wire
whisk 2 minutes. Let stand 5
minutes or until thickened. Stir in
whipped topping and ½ of
crushed cookies.

Place about 1 tablespoon crushed
cookies into each cup. Fill cups
about ¾ full with pudding
mixture. Top with remaining
crushed cookies.

Refrigerate until ready to serve.
Garnish just before serving.

Sand Cups: Use one package (12
ounces) vanilla wafer cookies and
JELL-O® Vanilla Flavor Instant
Pudding & Pie Filling.

Chocolate Peanut Butter Cups

Makes 30 servings

1 package DUNCAN HINES®
   Moist Deluxe® Swiss
   Chocolate Cake Mix
1 container DUNCAN HINES®
   Creamy Homestyle
   Vanilla Frosting
½ cup JIF® Creamy Peanut
   Butter
15 miniature peanut butter
   cup candies, wrappers
   removed, cut in half
   vertically

1. Preheat oven to 350°F. Place
30 (2½-inch) paper liners in
muffin cups.

2. Prepare, bake and cool
cupcakes following package
directions for basic recipe.

3. Combine Vanilla frosting and
peanut butter in medium bowl.
Stir until smooth. Frost one
cupcake. Decorate with peanut
butter cup candy, cut-side down.
Repeat with remaining cupcakes.

Peanut Butter Jumbos

Makes about 1½ dozen cookies

½ cup butter or margarine,
    softened
1 cup packed brown sugar
1 cup granulated sugar
1½ cups peanut butter
3 eggs
2 teaspoons baking soda
1 teaspoon vanilla
4½ cups uncooked rolled oats
1 cup (6 ounces) semisweet
    chocolate chips
1 cup candy-coated chocolate
    pieces

Preheat oven to 350°F. Lightly grease cookie sheets.

Beat butter, sugars, peanut butter and eggs in large bowl until well blended. Blend in baking soda, vanilla and oats until well mixed.

Stir in chocolate chips and candy pieces.

Scoop out about ⅓ cupful of dough for each cookie. Place on prepared cookie sheets, spacing about 4 inches apart. Press each cookie to flatten slightly. Bake 15 to 20 minutes or until firm in center. Remove to wire racks to cool.

Peanut Butter Jumbo Sandwiches: Prepare cookies as directed. Place ⅓ cup softened chocolate or vanilla ice cream on cookie bottom. Top with cookie. Lightly press sandwich together. Repeat with remaining cookies. Wrap sandwiches in plastic wrap; freeze until firm.

Cookie Pops

Makes 20 cookies

1 package (20 ounces)
    refrigerated sugar cookie
    dough
All-purpose flour (optional)
20 (4-inch) lollipop sticks
    Assorted colored sugars,
    frostings, glazes and gels

1. Preheat oven to 350°F. Grease cookie sheets.

2. Remove dough from wrapper according to package directions.

3. Sprinkle with flour to minimize sticking, if necessary. Cut dough in half. Reserve 1 half; refrigerate remaining dough.

4. Roll reserved dough to ⅛-inch thickness. Cut out cookies using 3½-inch cookie cutters.

5. Place lollipop sticks on cookies so that tips of sticks are imbedded in cookies. Carefully turn cookies so sticks are in back; place on prepared cookie sheets. Repeat with remaining dough.

6. Bake 7 to 11 minutes or until edges are lightly browned. Cool cookies on cookie sheets 2 minutes. Remove cookies to wire racks; cool completely.

7. Decorate with colored sugars, frostings, glazes and gels as desired.

Purple Cow Jumped Over the Moon

Milk shakes are all-time favorites with kids. Any one of these fruity low-fat shakes is sure to win raves.

Makes 8 (½-cup) servings

3 cups vanilla nonfat frozen yogurt
1 cup milk
½ cup thawed frozen grape juice concentrate (undiluted)
1½ teaspoons lemon juice

1. Place yogurt, milk, grape juice concentrate and lemon juice in food processor or blender container; process until smooth. Serve immediately.

Chocolate Rootbeer Shake: Place 1 quart vanilla nonfat frozen yogurt, 1 cup vanilla nonfat yogurt and ¼ cup chocolate nonfat syrup in food processor or blender container; process until smooth. Pour ½ of mixture evenly into 12 glasses; top with ½ of (12-ounce) can root beer. Fill glasses equally with remaining yogurt mixture; top with remaining root beer.

Makes 12 (⅔-cup) servings

Sunshine Shake: Place 1 quart vanilla nonfat frozen yogurt, 1⅓ cups orange juice, 1 cup fresh or thawed frozen raspberries and 1 teaspoon sugar in food processor or blender container; process until smooth. Pour into 10 glasses; sprinkle with ground nutmeg.

Makes 10 (½-cup) servings

Clown Cupcakes

Makes 12 clown cupcakes

1 package DUNCAN HINES® Yellow Cake Mix
12 scoops vanilla ice cream
12 sugar ice cream cones
1 container (7 ounces) refrigerated aerosol whipped cream
Assorted colored decors
Assorted candies for eyes, nose and mouth

1. Preheat oven to 350°F. Place 2½-inch paper liners in 24 muffin cups.

2. Prepare, bake and cool cupcakes following package directions.

3. Remove paper from cupcakes. Place top-side down on serving plates. Top with scoops of ice cream. Place cones on ice cream for hats. Spray whipped cream around bottom of cupcakes for collar. Spray three small dots up front on cones. Decorate faces with assorted colored decors.

Note: Freeze remaining cupcakes for later use.

Purple Cow Jumped Over the Moon

Mini Pizza Cookies

Makes 8 cookies

1 20-ounce tube prepared
   sugar cookie dough
2 cups (16 ounces) prepared
   pink frosting
   "M&M's"® Chocolate Mini
   Baking Bits
   "Pizza" toppings

Preheat oven to 350°F. Lightly grease cookie sheets; set aside. Divide dough into 8 equal portions. On lightly floured surface, roll each portion of dough into ¼-inch-thick circle; place about 2 inches apart onto prepared cookie sheets. Bake 10 to 13 minutes or until golden brown on edges. Cool completely on wire racks. Spread top of each pizza with frosting; sprinkle with "M&M's"® Chocolate Mini Baking Bits and 2 or 3 "pizza" toppings.

Rainbows

Makes about 5 dozen cookies

2¼ cups all-purpose flour
 ¼ teaspoon salt
 1 cup sugar
 ¾ cup butter, softened
 1 egg
 1 teaspoon vanilla
 1 teaspoon almond extract
   Red, green, yellow and blue
      paste food colors
   White frosting and yellow
      sugar sprinkles

Combine flour and salt. Beat sugar and butter in large bowl until fluffy. Beat in egg, vanilla and extract. Add flour mixture. Beat until well blended. Divide dough into 10 equal sections.

Blend 4 sections dough and red food color, 3 sections dough and green food color, 2 sections dough and yellow food color, and remaining dough and blue food color. Refrigerate 30 minutes.

Shape blue dough into 8-inch log. Shape yellow dough into 8×3-inch rectangle; place on waxed paper. Place blue log in center of yellow rectangle. Fold yellow edges up and around blue log, pinching to seal. Roll to form smooth log.

Roll green dough into 8×5-inch rectangle on waxed paper. Place yellow log in center of green rectangle. Fold green edges up and around yellow log. Pinch to seal. Roll gently to form smooth log. Roll red dough into 8×7-inch rectangle. Place green log in center of red rectangle. Fold red edges up and around green log. Pinch to seal. Roll gently to form smooth log. Wrap in plastic wrap. Refrigerate 1 hour.

Preheat oven to 350°F. Grease cookie sheets. Cut log in half lengthwise. Cut each half into ¼-inch-thick slices. Place slices 1 inch apart on prepared cookie sheets. Bake 8 to 12 minutes. *(Do not brown.)* Cool on cookie sheets 1 minute. Remove to wire racks; cool completely. Pipe small amount of frosting on each cookie; sprinkle with sugar.

Mini Pizza Cookies

It's Snack Time!

One Potato, Two Potato

Having a tough time getting your child to eat enough potatoes? After sampling these crispy low-fat potato wedges, the kids will be begging for more!

Makes 4 servings

Nonstick cooking spray
2 medium baking potatoes, cut lengthwise into 4 wedges
Salt
½ cup unseasoned dry bread crumbs
2 tablespoons grated Parmesan cheese (optional)
1½ teaspoons dried oregano leaves, dill weed, Italian herbs or paprika
Spicy brown or honey mustard, ketchup or reduced-fat sour cream

1. Preheat oven to 425°F. Spray baking sheet with nonstick cooking spray; set aside.

2. Spray cut sides of potatoes generously with cooking spray; sprinkle lightly with salt.

3. Combine bread crumbs, Parmesan cheese and desired herb in shallow dish. Add potatoes; toss lightly until potatoes are generously coated with crumb mixture. Place on prepared baking sheet.

4. Bake potatoes until browned and tender, about 20 minutes. Serve warm as dippers with mustard.

Potato Sweets: Omit Parmesan cheese, herbs and mustard. Substitute sweet potatoes for baking potatoes. Cut and spray potatoes as directed; coat generously with desired amount of cinnamon-sugar. Bake as directed. Serve warm as dippers with peach or pineapple preserves or honey mustard.

One Potato, Two Potato

Tex-Mex Chicken Fingers

Makes 12 appetizers

½ cup dried bread crumbs or cracker crumbs
2 tablespoons all-purpose flour
1 teaspoon chili powder
½ teaspoon salt
¼ teaspoon ground cumin
1 pound (about 12) boneless chicken tenderloins
2 eggs, lightly beaten
3 to 4 tablespoons vegetable oil
ORTEGA® Green Chile Picante Sauce, mild

COMBINE crumbs, flour, chili powder, salt and cumin in small shallow bowl.

DIP chicken in eggs; coat with crumb mixture.

HEAT oil in large skillet over medium-high heat. Add chicken; cook for 5 to 6 minutes or until golden brown on outside and no longer pink in center. Serve with picante sauce for dipping.

Bite-Size Tacos

Makes 8 appetizer servings

1 pound ground beef
1 package (1.25 ounces) taco seasoning mix
¾ cup water
1⅓ cups (2.8-ounce can) FRENCH'S® French Fried Onions, divided
¼ cup chopped fresh cilantro
32 bite-size round tortilla chips
¾ cup low-fat sour cream
⅓ cup shredded Cheddar cheese

Preheat oven to 350°F. Prepare taco mixture according to package directions using ground beef, seasoning mix and water. Stir in ⅔ cup French Fried Onions and cilantro.

Arrange tortilla chips on foil-lined baking sheet. Spread each chip with 1 tablespoon beef mixture and 1 teaspoon sour cream. Sprinkle evenly with cheese and remaining ⅔ cup onions.

Bake 5 minutes or until cheese melts and onions are golden.

PREP TIME: 20 minutes
COOK TIME: 15 minutes

Tex-Mex Chicken Fingers

Nachos à la Ortega®

Makes 4 to 6 servings

1¾ cups (1-pound can) ORTEGA® Refried Beans, heated
4 cups (4 ounces) tortilla chips
1½ cups (6 ounces) shredded Cheddar or Monterey Jack cheese
¼ cup ORTEGA® Sliced Jalapeños
ORTEGA® Thick & Chunky Salsa, hot, medium or mild
Sour cream
Additional topping suggestions: guacamole, sliced ripe olives, chopped green onions, chopped fresh cilantro

SPREAD beans onto bottom of large ovenproof platter or jelly-roll pan. Arrange chips over beans. Top with cheese and jalapeños.

PLACE under preheated broiler, 4 inches from heat source, for 1 to 1½ minutes or until cheese is melted. Top with salsa, sour cream and additional toppings, if desired.

Baked Mozzarella Sticks

Makes 12 cheese sticks

Butter-flavored nonstick cooking spray
12 ounces (2 blocks) ALPINE LACE® Fat Free Pasteurized Process Skim Milk Cheese Product— For Mozzarella Lovers
½ cup egg substitute or 2 large eggs
1 cup Italian seasoned dry bread crumbs
¼ cup minced fresh parsley

1. Preheat the oven to 400°F. Spray 2 large baking sheets with the cooking spray.

2. Cut each block of cheese in half crosswise, then each half lengthwise into 3 equal sticks (about 3×¾ inches), making a total of 12 sticks.

3. In a medium-size bowl, whisk the egg substitute (or the whole eggs) until frothy. On a plate, toss the bread crumbs with the parsley.

4. Dip each cheese stick first into the egg substitute, then roll in the bread crumbs, pressing them slightly as you go. Arrange the cheese in a single layer on the baking sheets.

5. Spray the sticks lightly with the cooking spray. Bake for 10 minutes or until golden brown and crispy.

Nachos à la Ortega®

Soft Pretzels

Makes 8 servings

1 package (16 ounces) hot roll mix plus ingredients to prepare mix
1 egg white
2 teaspoons water
2 tablespoons *each* assorted coatings: grated Parmesan cheese, sesame seeds, poppy seeds, dried oregano leaves

1. Prepare hot roll mix according to package directions.

2. Preheat oven to 375°F. Spray baking sheets with nonstick cooking spray; set aside.

3. Divide dough equally into 16 pieces; roll each piece with hands to form a rope, 7 to 10 inches long. Place on prepared cookie sheets; form into desired shape (hearts, wreaths, pretzels, snails, loops, etc.).

4. Beat together egg white and water in small bowl until foamy.

Brush onto dough shapes; sprinkle each shape with 1½ teaspoons of one of the coatings.

5. Bake until golden brown, about 15 minutes. Serve warm or at room temperature.

Fruit Twists: Omit coatings. Prepare dough and roll into ropes as directed. Place ropes on lightly floured surface. Roll out, or pat, each rope into rectangle, ¼ inch thick; brush each rectangle with about 1 teaspoon spreadable fruit or preserves. Fold each rectangle lengthwise in half; twist into desired shape. Bake as directed.

Cheese Twists: Omit coatings. Prepare dough and roll into rectangles as directed in Fruit Twists. Sprinkle each rectangle with about 1 tablespoon shredded Cheddar or other flavor cheese. Fold dough rectangles, shape and bake as directed for Fruit Twists.

Take-Along Snack Mix

Makes about 3½ cups

1 tablespoon butter or margarine
2 tablespoons honey
1 cup toasted oat cereal, any flavor
½ cup coarsely broken pecans
½ cup thin pretzel sticks, broken in half
½ cup raisins
1 cup "M&M's"® Chocolate Mini Baking Bits

In large heavy skillet over low heat, melt butter; add honey and stir until blended. Add cereal, nuts, pretzels and raisins, stirring until all pieces are evenly coated. Continue cooking over low heat about 10 minutes, stirring frequently. Remove from heat; immediately spread on waxed paper until cool. Add "M&M's"® Chocolate Mini Baking Bits. Store in tightly covered container.

Soft Pretzels

Picnic Pizza Biscuits

Makes 10 servings

1 can (10 ounces)
   refrigerated buttermilk
   biscuits
1 pound hot Italian sausage,
   casings removed
½ cup chopped onion
½ cup sliced mushrooms
½ cup chopped green bell
   pepper
½ cup (2 ounces) shredded
   mozzarella cheese
¼ cup marinara or pizza sauce
2 tablespoons FRENCH'S®
   Dijon Mustard

1. Preheat oven to 375°F.
Separate biscuits; pat or roll into
10 (4-inch) circles on floured
surface. Press circles into 12-cup
muffin pan.

2. Cook sausage in large nonstick
skillet over high heat 5 minutes
or until browned, stirring to
separate meat; drain fat. Add
onion, mushrooms and bell
pepper; cook and stir 3 minutes
or until vegetables are tender. Stir
in cheese, sauce and mustard;
mix well.

3. Mound filling evenly in
biscuits. Bake 20 minutes or until
biscuits are browned. Serve warm
or at room temperature.

PREP TIME: 30 minutes
COOK TIME: 25 minutes

Buffalo Bar-B-Q Nuggets

Makes 6 to 8 servings

½ cup FRANK'S® Original
   REDHOT® Cayenne
   Pepper Sauce
⅓ cup butter, melted
1½ pounds boneless skinless
   chicken thighs or breasts
   Lettuce leaves
   Blue cheese salad dressing
   (optional)

1. Combine RedHot® sauce and
butter in small bowl; mix well.
Reserve ⅓ cup sauce mixture.
Pour remaining sauce over
chicken. Cover; refrigerate 20
minutes. Prepare grill.

2. Remove chicken; discard
remaining marinade. Place
chicken on oiled grid. Grill, over
medium coals, about 10 minutes
or until no longer pink in center.
Heat reserved sauce. Cut chicken
into bite-size pieces; toss chicken
pieces in warmed sauce.

3. Arrange chicken on lettuce-
lined serving platter. Serve with
blue cheese dressing, if desired.

PREP TIME: 10 minutes
MARINATE TIME: 20 minutes
COOK TIME: 10 minutes

Picnic Pizza Biscuits